FLOWERS FOR

My Mother

RASHIDA TAHIRAH

FLOWERS FOR MY MOTHER

Acknowledgements

This book is dedicated to my mother Cynthia O. Fauntleroy who birthed in me the gift of reading and cultivated the skill of writing.

I love and miss you to infinity!

I also wish to acknowledge those who have taught me the value of patience and the lessons on forgiveness.
Thank You!

Special thank you to DLM for the inspiration!

Flowers

Flowers are the gift that keeps on giving. I gave my mother flowers for every special occasion. They became a welcomed treat that she always looked forward to. My mother transitioned in December of 2017. Life has not been the same without her. One of the things I miss most is not being able to give her flowers. This book is meant to serve as one final "gift" to my mother. One last bouquet of "flowers". I have crafted 10 "pillars" or "petals" that represent her. Under each one I have included some of her favorite scriptures, proverbs and affirmations. They say you should give a person their flowers while they are living but, I think this one exception will be ok!

Enjoy!

God

"O Lord, thou art my God; I will exalt thee, I will praise thy name; for thou hast done wonderful things; thy counsels of old are faithfulness and truth."

—Isaiah 25:1 | KJV

"The calamity that makes you remember God is better than the blessings that made you forget God."

—African Proverb

God

God or the concept of God was something my mother was grounded and rooted in. She was raised under a traditional Protestant path of Methodism. Her young adulthood was spent exploring alternative views. She became a Muslim and followed the tenants of Islam for several years. After careful examination of the traditions, philosophy and practices behind traditional religion she began to investigate other things. She was led to more esoteric views and traditional African spiritual systems. What I learned about God from my mother is that there are many paths to God. The path chosen is unique to each individual. I also learned that the path you choose is not important, it is the journey on the path that matters.

God

The Word Says:

"But if from thence thou shalt seek the Lord thy God, thou shalt find him, if thou seek him with all thy heart and with all thy soul."

—Deuteronomy 4:29 | KJV

The Ancestors Say:

"The plant God favors grows without rain."

—African Proverb

Affirmation

"I will trust God!"

God

The Word Says:

"For I the Lord thy God will hold thy right hand, saying unto thee, Fear not; I will help thee."

—Isaiah 41:13 | KJV

The Ancestors Say:

"When God cooks you don't see smoke."

—African Proverb

Affirmation

"I will trust God!"

God

The Word Says:

"The Lord thy God in the midst of thee is mighty; he will save, he will rejoice over thee with joy; he will rest in his love, he will joy over thee with singing."

−Zephaniah 3:17 | KJV

The Ancestors Say:

"God does not bless mess."

−African Proverb

Affirmation

"I will trust God!"

God

The Word Says:

"And we have known and believed the love that God hath to us. God is love; and he that dwelleth in love dwelleth in God, and God in him."

—1 John 4:16 | KJV

The Ancestors Say:

"God is good but never dance with a lion."

—African Proverb

Affirmation

"I will trust God!"

God

The Word Says:

"Wherefore thou art great, O Lord God: for there is none like thee, neither is there any God beside thee, according to all that we have heard with our ears."

−2 Samuel 7:22 | KJV

The Ancestors Say:

"When one is in trouble one remembers God."

−African Proverb

Affirmation

"I will trust God!"

God

The Word Says:

"For every house is built by some man; but he that built all things is God."

—Hebrews 3:4 | KJV

The Ancestors Say:

"Do not blame God for having created the tiger, but thank him for not giving it wings."

—African Proverb

Affirmation

"I will trust God!"

God

The Word Says:

"Be not deceived; God is not mocked: for whatsoever a man soweth, that shall he also reap."

–Galatians 6:7 | KJV

The Ancestors Say

"When you throw a stone at God it lands on top of your head."

–African Proverb

Affirmation

"I will trust God!"

God

The Word Says:

"If a man say, I love God, and hateth his brother, he is a liar: for he that loveth not his brother whom he hath seen, how can he love God whom he hath not seen?"

—1 John 4:20 | KJV

The Ancestors Say:

"No one has to point God out to you child."

—African Proverb

Affirmation

"I will trust God!"

God

The Word Says:

"No man hath seen God at any time. If we love one another, God dwelleth in us, and his love is perfected in us."

—1 John 4:12 | KJV

The Ancestors Say:

"God gives nothing to the man with his arms crossed."

—African Proverb

Affirmation

"I will trust God!"

God

The Word Says:

"There is none holy as the Lord: for there is none beside thee: neither is there any rock like our God."

–1 Samuel 2:2 | KJV

The Ancestors Say:

"When you stand with the blessings of God and your mother it matters not who stands against you."

–African Proverb

Affirmation

"I will trust God!"

Truth

"He that walketh uprightly, and worketh righteousness, and speaketh the truth in his heart. He that backbiteth not with his tongue, nor doeth evil to his neighbor, nor taketh up a reproach against his neighbor."

—Psalms 15:2-| KJV

"All truth is good but not all truth is good to say."

—African Proverb

Truth

Truth was the essence of who my mother was. Truth for her was a way of life. This way of being and existing involved many facets of the concept of truth. Not only was it important that she told the truth but it was also of utmost importance to her that she sought the truth in all matters. In this way she was a truth seeker. Wanting to know and understand the truth led her down many roads. "Dealing only in truth" makes you unpopular, not liked and judged. What she taught me about the truth that was most important is that you must live from your truth at all times.

Truth

The Word Says:

"Lying lips are abomination to the LORD: but they that deal truly are his delight."

−Proverbs 12:22 | KJV

The Ancestors Say:

"A speaker of the truth has no friends."

−African Proverb

Affirmation

"I only deal in Truth."

Truth

The Word Says:

"If we say that we have fellowship with him, and walk in darkness, we lie, and do not the truth:"

–1 John 1:6 | KJV

The Ancestors Say:

"Love Truth even if it hurts you and hate lies even if they help you."

–African Proverb

Affirmation

"I only deal in Truth."

Truth

The Word Says:

"Then said Jesus to those Jews which believed on him, If ye continue in my word, then are ye my disciples indeed; And ye shall know the truth, and the truth shall make you free."

−John 8:31-32 | KJV

The Ancestors Say:

"Whoever tells the truth is chased out of nine villages."

−African Proverb

Affirmation

"I only deal in Truth."

Truth

The Word Says:

"Finally, brethren, whatsoever things are true, whatsoever things are honest, whatsoever things are just, whatsoever things are pure, whatsoever things are lovely, whatsoever things are of good report; if there be any virtue, and if there be any praise, think on these things."

–Philippians 4:8 | KJV

The Ancestors Say:

"A lie has many variations the Truth none."

–African Proverb

Affirmation

"I only deal in Truth."

Truth

The Word Says:

"Jesus saith unto him, I am the way, the truth, and the life: no man cometh unto the Father, but by me."

—John 14:6 | KJV

The Ancestors Say:

"The Truth passes through fire and does not burn."

—African Proverb

Affirmation

"I only deal in Truth."

Truth

The Word Says:

"Study to shew thyself approved unto God, a workman that needeth not to be ashamed, rightly dividing the word of truth."

—2 Timothy 2:15 | KJV

The Ancestors Say:

"One falsehood spoils a thousand Truths."

—African Proverb

Affirmation

"I only deal in Truth."

Truth

The Word Says:

"God is a Spirit: and they that worship him must worship him in spirit and in truth."

—John 4:24 | KJV

The Ancestors Say:

"Truth is the first victim of war."

—African Proverb

Affirmation

"I only deal in Truth."

Truth

The Word Says:

"Of his own will begat he us with the word of truth, that we should be a kind of first fruits of his creatures."

—James 1:18 | KJV

The Ancestors Say:

"A lie can travel half way around the world while the truth is still putting on its shoes."

—African Proverb

Affirmation

"I only deal in Truth."

Truth

The Word Says:

"And we know that the Son of God is come, and hath given us an understanding, that we may know him that is true, and we are in him that is true, even in his Son Jesus Christ. This is the true God, and eternal life."

−1 John 5:20 |KJV

The Ancestors Say:

"The words you say to tell the Truth are as important as the decision to be Truthful."

−African Proverb

Affirmation

"I only deal in Truth."

Truth

The Word Says:

"My little children, let us not love in word, neither in tongue; but in deed and in truth."

−1 John 3:18 |KJV

The Ancestors Say:

"The naked Truth is always better than the best dressed lie."

−African Proverb

Affirmation

"I only deal in Truth."

Love

"That he would grant you, according to the riches of his glory, to be strengthened with might by his Spirit in the inner man; that Christ may dwell in your hearts by faith; that ye, being rooted and grounded in love."

—Ephesians 3:16-17 |KJV

"Don't be so in love that you can't tell when it's raining."

—African Proverb

Love

Love was a practical matter for my mother. Her mother passed away when she was very young. The absence of a mother's love would affect her very deeply throughout her life. Although she received love from the family that was left to raise her, she did not receive the maternal love that a child needs. Love for her was more about respect and provision. It was very simple, if you wanted to show her love then you moved in a respectful manner. She showed her love through providing for you. What I learned from my mother about love is to love fearlessly. What she also taught me is to be willing to lay it all on the line for love. Lastly she showed me that you will always receive the love you need even if it is not from the person you gave it to.

Love

The Word Says:

"But as it is written, Eye hath not seen, nor ear heard, neither have entered into the heart of man, the things which God hath prepared for them that love him."

—1 Corinthians 2:9 |KJV

The Ancestors Say:

"When one is in love, a cliff becomes a meadow."

—African Proverb

Affirmation

"Love yourself first!"

Love

The Word Says:

"For the love of Christ constraineth us; because we thus judge, that if one died for all, then were all dead:"

−2 Corinthians 5:14 | KJV

The Ancestors Say:

"Love is a painkiller."

−African Proverb

Affirmation

"Love yourself first!"

Love

The Word Says:

"For out of much affliction and anguish of heart I wrote unto you with many tears; not that ye should be grieved, but that ye might know the love which I have more abundantly unto you."

−2 Corinthians 2:4 |KJV

The Ancestors Say:

"Where there is love, there is no darkness."

−African Proverb

Affirmation

"Love yourself first!"

Love

The Word Says:

"And we have known and believed the love that God hath to us. God is love; and he that dwelleth in love dwelleth in God, and God in him."

—1 John 4:16 |KJV

The Ancestors Say:

"He who loves, love you with your dirt."

—African Proverb

Affirmation

"Love yourself first!"

Love

The Word Says:

"With all lowliness and meekness, with longsuffering, forbearing one another in love."

—Ephesians 4:2 |KJV

The Ancestors Say:

"Love doesn't rely on physical features."

—African Proverb

Affirmation

"Love yourself first!"

Love

The Word Says:

"We love him, because he first loved us."

-1 John 4:19 |KJV

The Ancestors Say:

"Even as the archer loves the arrow that flies, so too he loves the bow that remains constant in his hands."

-African Proverb

Affirmation

"Love yourself first!"

Love

The Word Says:

"And this I pray, that your love may abound yet more and more in knowledge and in all judgment;"

−Philippians 1:9|KJV

The Ancestors Say:

"To love someone who does not love you is like shaking a tree to make the dew drops fall."

−African Proverb

Affirmation

"Love yourself first!"

Love

The Word Says:

"That their hearts might be comforted, being knit together in love, and unto all riches of the full assurance of understanding, to the acknowledgement of the mystery of God, and of the Father, and of Christ."

–Colossians 2:2 |KJV

The Ancestors Say:

"The quarrel of lovers is the renewal of love."

–African Proverb

Affirmation

"Love yourself first!"

Love

The Word Says:

"Let love be without dissimulation. Abhor that which is evil; cleave to that which is good."

—Romans 12:9 | KJV

The Ancestors Say:

"If the full moon loves you, why worry about the stars?"

—African Proverb

Affirmation

"Love yourself first!"

Love

The Word Says:

"And the Lord direct your hearts into the love of God, and into the patient waiting for Christ."

–2 Thessalonians 3:5 |KJV

The Ancestors Say:

"Love, like rain, does not choose the grass on which it falls."

–African Proverb

Affirmation

"Love yourself first!"

Hope

"What is my strength, that I should hope? and what is mine end, that I should prolong my life?"

—Job 6:11 |KJV

"While there is life there is Hope."

—African Proverb

Hope

Hope was how my mother coped with life. She attempted to remain hopeful always. No matter what she faced in life, her unending optimism always pulled her through. She often paired her hope with her lofty dreams. She hoped that if she did not accomplish everything she wanted in this physical life that it would still happen. Her hope was built on the foundation of her relationship with God. What she taught me about hope that was most important is never to lose it. Hope provides the assurance that things are never as bad as they seem, and that they will always get better.

Hope

The Word Says:

"Why art thou cast down, O my soul? and why art thou disquieted within me? hope thou in God: for I shall yet praise him, who is the health of my countenance, and my God."

–Psalm 42:11 |KJV

The Ancestors Say:

"If you are rich in hope do not make a baboon your friend."

–African Proverb

Affirmation

"I will remain Hopeful!"

Hope

The Word Says:

"But I will hope continually, and will yet praise thee more and more."

—Psalms 71:14 |KJV

The Ancestors Say:

"Where there is hope there is no darkness."

—African Proverb

Affirmation

"I will remain Hopeful!"

Hope

The Word Says:

"Now the God of hope fill you with all joy and peace in believing, that ye may abound in hope, through the power of the Holy Ghost."

—Romans 15:13 | KJV

The Ancestors Say:

"Hope is the pillar of the world."

—African Proverb

Affirmation

"I will remain Hopeful!"

Hope

The Word Says:

"And not only so, but we glory in tribulations also: knowing that tribulation worketh patience and patience, experience; and experience, hope."

–Romans 5:3-4 |KJV

The Ancestors Say:

"A little hope each day can fill the rivers to flowing."

–African Proverb

Affirmation

"I will remain Hopeful!"

Hope

The Word Says:

"Thou art my hiding place and my shield: I hope in thy word."

—Psalm 119:114 | KJV

The Ancestors Say:

"Your greatest hope is your greatest fear."

—African Proverb

Affirmation

"I will remain Hopeful!"

Hope

The Word Says:

"And there is hope in thine end, saith the LORD, that thy children shall come again to their own border."

—Jeremiah 31:11 | KJV

The Ancestors Say:

"With a little seed of imagination, you can grow a field of hope."

—African Proverb

Affirmation

"I will remain Hopeful!"

Hope

The Word Says:

"All that found them have devoured them: and their adversaries said, We offend not, because they have sinned against the LORD, the habitation of justice, even the LORD, the hope of their fathers. "The Word Says: Be strong and take heart, all you who hope in the Lord."

–Jeremiah 50:7|KJV

The Ancestors Say:

"Hope is a good thing and good things never die."

–African Proverb

Affirmation

"I will remain Hopeful!"

Hope

The Word Says:

"The Lord also shall roar out of Zion, and utter his voice from Jerusalem; and the heavens and the earth shall shake: but the Lord will be the hope of his people, and the strength of the children of Israel."

–Joel 3:16 |KJV

The Ancestors Say:

"The smaller the lizard the greater the hope of becoming a crocodile."

–African Proverb

Affirmation

"I will remain Hopeful!"

Hope

The Word Says:

"And if ye lend to them of whom ye hope to receive, what thank have ye? for sinners also lend to sinners, to receive as much again."

—Luke 6:34 | KJV

The Ancestors Say:

"What one hopes for is always better then what one has."

—African Proverb

Affirmation

"I will remain Hopeful!"

Hope

The Word Says:

"And when neither sun nor stars in many days appeared, and no small tempest lay on us, all hope that we should be saved was then taken away."

–Acts 27:20 |KJV

The Ancestors Say:

"Hope does not kill; I shall live in hope of getting what I seek another day."

–African Proverb

Affirmation

"I will remain Hopeful!"

Blessings

"Blessed is the man that trusteth in the LORD, and whose hope the LORD is. For he shall be as a tree planted by the waters, and [that] spreadeth out her roots by the river, and shall not see when heat cometh, but her leaf shall be green; and shall not be careful in the year of drought, neither shall cease from yielding fruit."

—Jeremiah 17:7-8 |KJV

"Every misfortune is a blessing."

—African Proverb

Blessings

Blessings were always surely lurking around the corner in my mother's eyes. She often told me that life was sometimes feast or famine. There would always be lean times but, these times would always be followed by bountiful overflowing blessings. There were many other things she taught me about blessings. Among these things were to recognize the blessing no matter how big or small, and to always be grateful when it showed up. I also learned that we are blessed so that we can be a blessing to others.

Blessings

The Word Says:

"The LORD bless thee, and keep thee: The LORD make his face shine upon thee, and be gracious unto thee: The LORD lift up his countenance upon thee, and give thee peace."

—Numbers 6:24-26 |KJV

The Ancestors Say:

"Blessings of ancestors are greater than those of a living human being."

—African Proverb

Affirmation

"I will walk in Blessings!"

Blessings

The Word Says:

"O taste and see that the LORD is good: blessed is the man that trusteth in him."

—Psalm 34:8|KJV

The Ancestors Say:

"He who wakes up early in the morning receives a bundle of blessings."

—African Proverb

Affirmation

"I will walk in Blessings!"

Blessings

The Word Says:

"And ye shall serve the Lord your God, and he shall bless thy bread, and thy water; and I will take sickness away from the midst of thee."

−Exodus 23:25 |KJV

The Ancestors Say:

"When you stand with the blessings of your mother and God, it matters not who stands against you."

−African Proverb

Affirmation

"I will walk in Blessings!"

Blessings

The Word Says:

"Bless them which persecute you: bless, and curse not."

—Romans 12:14 | KJV

The Ancestors Say:

"A deaf ear is followed by death; an ear that listens is followed by blessings."

—African Proverb

Affirmation

"I will walk in Blessings!"

Blessings

The Word Says:

"And God blessed them, and God said unto them, Be fruitful, and multiply, and replenish the earth, and subdue it: and have dominion over the fish of the sea, and over the fowl of the air, and over every living thing that moveth upon the earth."

—Genesis 1:28 | KJV

The Ancestors Say:

"Every delay has its blessings."

—African Proverbs

Affirmation

"I will walk in Blessings!"

Blessings

The Word Says:

"And they blessed Rebekah, and said unto her, Thou art our sister, be thou the mother of thousands of millions, and let thy seed possess the gate of those which hate them."

—Genesis 24:60 |KJV

The Ancestors Say:

"Give thanks for unknown blessings already on their way."

—African Proverb

Affirmation

"I will walk in Blessings!"

Blessings

The Word Says:

"And I will make thy seed to multiply as the stars of heaven, and will give unto thy seed all these countries; and in thy seed shall all the nations of the earth be blessed."

–Genesis 26:4| NIV

The Ancestors Say:

"Blessings of ancestors are greater than those of a living human being."

–African Proverb

Affirmation

"I will walk in Blessings!"

Blessings

The Word Says:

"Bring ye all the tithes into the storehouse, that there may be meat in mine house, and prove me now herewith, saith the Lord of hosts, if I will not open you the windows of heaven, and pour you out a blessing, that there shall not be room enough to receive it."

–Malachi 3:10 |KJV

The Ancestors Say:

"The calamity that makes you remember God is better than the blessings that make you forget God."

–African Proverb

Affirmation

"I will walk in Blessings!"

Blessings

The Word Says:

"Blessed are the peacemakers, for they will be called children of God."

—Matthew 5:9 |KJV

The Ancestors Say:

"Train yourself to find the blessing in everything."

—African Proverb

Affirmation

"I will walk in Blessings!"

Blessings

The Word Says:

"Blessed are they that keep his testimonies, and that seek him with the whole heart."

—Psalm 119:2 |KJV

The Ancestors Say:

"Hurry, hurry has no blessings."

—African Proverb

Affirmation

"I will walk in Blessings!"

Faith

"That he would grant you, according to the riches of his glory, to be strengthened with might by his Spirit in the inner man; That Christ may dwell in your hearts by faith; that ye, being rooted and grounded in love."

−Ephesians 3:16-17 | KJV

"When you pray move your feet."

−African Proverb

Faith

Faith was another foundational principal that made my mother who she was. She was girded in faith at all times. When the world came crashing down around her she always kept the faith. She had faith in God but, she also had faith in her ability to deal with situations. She taught me to have faith and to also be faithful to the things I enter into. I also learned to have faith despite what things look like. Things often appear as if they are not moving in the direction we would like. Faith provides the assurance that they will still turn out in our favor. The most important thing my mother taught me about faith is to have it even when you don't feel like it!

Faith

The Word Says:

"Now faith is the substance of things hoped for, the evidence of things not seen."

—Hebrews 11:1 | KJV

The Ancestors Say:

"Do not stand in a place of danger trusting miracles."

—African Proverb

Affirmation

"I will have Faith!"

Faith

The Word Says:

"For we walk by faith, not by sight."

−2 Corinthians 5:7 | KJV

The Ancestors Say:

"However long the night the dawn will break."

−African Proverb

Affirmation

"I will have Faith!"

Faith

The Word Says:

"But let him ask in faith, nothing wavering. For he that wavereth is like a wave of the sea driven with the wind and tossed."

—James 1:6 | KJV

The Ancestors Say:

"Where there is faith there is no darkness."

—African Proverb

Affirmation

"I will have Faith!"

Faith

The Word Says:

"But without faith it is impossible to please him: for he that cometh to God must believe that he is, and that he is a rewarder of them that diligently seek him."

—Hebrews 11:6 | KJV

The Ancestors Say:

"A man is taller than every mountain he climbs."

—African Proverb

Affirmation

"I will have Faith!"

Faith

The Word Says:

"Whom having not seen, ye love; in whom, though now ye see him not, yet believing, ye rejoice with joy unspeakable and full of glory: Receiving the end of your faith, even the salvation of your souls."

−1 Peter 1:8-9 | KJV

The Ancestors Say:

"However long the night, the dawn will break."

−African Proverbs

Affirmation

"I will have Faith!"

Faith

The Word Says:

"For whatsoever is born of God over cometh the world: and this is the victory that over cometh the world, even our faith."

—1 John 5:4 | KJV

The Ancestors Say:

"When a home is burnt down the rebuilt home is more beautiful."

—African Proverb

Affirmation

"I will have Faith!"

Faith

The Word Says:

"But thou, O man of God, flee these things; and follow after righteousness, godliness, faith, love, patience, meekness."

—1 Timothy 6:11 | KJV

The Ancestors Say:

"When Heaven is pointed out a fool only sees the tip of the finger."

—African Proverb

Affirmation

"I will have Faith!"

Faith

The Word Says:

"And Jesus said unto him, Go thy way; thy faith hath made thee whole. And immediately he received his sight, and followed Jesus in the way."

−Mark 10:52 | KJV

The Ancestors Say:

"Those that plan without the help of spirit must plan again."

−African Proverb

Affirmation

"I will have Faith!"

Faith

The Word Says:

"And though I have the gift of prophecy, and understand all mysteries, and all knowledge; and though I have all faith, so that I could remove mountains, and have not charity, I am nothing."

—1 Corinthians 13:2 | KJV

The Ancestors Say:

"If there's a Goliath in front of you then there is a David inside you."

—African Proverb

Affirmation

"I will have Faith!"

Faith

The Word Says:

"For therein is the righteousness of God revealed from faith to faith: as it is written, The just shall live by faith."

–Romans 1:17 | KJV

The Ancestors Say:

"An ant on its feet can do more than an elephant lying down."

–African Proverb

Affirmation

"I will have Faith!"

Courage

"Have not I commanded thee? Be strong and of a good courage; be not afraid, neither be thou dismayed: for the Lord thy God is with thee wherever thou goest."

—Joshua 1:9 | KJV

"An army is driven back by courage not by insults however many."

—African Proverb

Courage

My mother was a very strong person. She lived her life in a manner where she boldly looked fear in the face and laughed. She wore her courage like a plate of armor. There were many times in her life when she could have raised the white flag and given up but she didn't. She always kept moving. She would often say that sometimes you have to take one step backwards in order to take two steps forward. Regardless of the direction she was moving in she always moved fearlessly. What I learned most about courage from my mother came at the end of her life. Through her process of transition she taught me that it takes courage to live but it also takes courage to die.

Courage

The Word Says:

"And the Lord, he it is that doth go before thee; he will be with thee, he will not fail thee, neither forsake thee: fear not, neither be dismayed."

—Deuteronomy 31:8 | KJV

The Ancestors Say:

"A warrior fights with courage not anger."

—African Proverb

Affirmation

"I am Courageous."

Courage

The Word Says:

"Blessed be God, even the Father of our Lord Jesus Christ, the Father of mercies, and the God of all comfort; Who comforteth us in all our tribulation, that we may be able to comfort them which are in any trouble, by the comfort wherewith we ourselves are comforted of God."

—2 Corinthians 1:3-4 | KJV

The Ancestors Say:

"The lion doesn't turn around when the small dog barks."

—African Proverb

Affirmation

"I am Courageous."

Courage

The Word Says:

"Watch ye, stand fast in the faith, quit you like men, be strong."

−1 Corinthians 16:13 | KJV

The Ancestors Say:

"One cannot stop sleeping because of a fear of bad dreams."

−African Proverb

Affirmation

"I am Courageous."

Courage

The Word Says:

"Be of good courage, and he shall strengthen your heart, all ye that hope in the Lord."

—Psalm 31:24 | KJV

The Ancestors Say:

"The lion and the sheep may lay down together but the sheep won't get any sleep."

—African Proverb

Affirmation

"I am Courageous."

Courage

The Word Says:

"For God hath not given us the spirit of fear; but of power, and of love, and of a sound mind."

-2 Timothy 1:7 | KJV

The Ancestors Say:

"He who looks for honey must have the courage to face the bees."

—African Proverb

Affirmation

"I am Courageous."

Courage

The Word Says:

"Yea, though I walk through the valley of the shadow of death, I will fear no evil: for thou art with me; thy rod and thy staff they comfort me."

—Psalm 23:4 | KJV

The Ancestors Say:

"Courage, will, knowledge and silence are essential qualities for those on the path of perfection."

—African Proverb

Affirmation

"I am Courageous."

Courage

The Word Says:

"Peace I leave with you, my peace I give unto you: not as the world giveth, give I unto you. Let not your heart be troubled, neither let it be afraid."

—John 14:27 | KJV

The Ancestors Say:

"Don't think there are no crocodiles just because the water is calm."

—African Proverb

Affirmation

"I am Courageous."

Courage

The Word Says:

"Be strong and of a good courage, fear not, nor be afraid of them: for the Lord thy God, he it is that doth go with thee; he will not fail thee, nor forsake thee."

–Deuteronomy 31:6 | KJV

The Ancestors Say:

"Do not follow a person who is running away."

–African Proverb

Affirmation

"I am Courageous."

Courage

The Word Says:

"Wait on the Lord: be of good courage, and he shall strengthen thine heart: wait, I say, on the Lord."

—Psalm 27:14 | KJV

The Ancestors Say:

"There are three friends in this world: courage, sense and insight."

—African Proverb

Affirmation

"I am Courageous."

Courage

The Word Says:

"But when they saw him walking upon the sea, they supposed it had been a spirit, and cried out: For they all saw him, and were troubled. And immediately he talked with them, and saith unto them, Be of good cheer: it is I; be not afraid."

—Mark 6:49-50 | KJV

The Ancestors Say:

"When there is no enemy within, the enemy outside can't hurt you."

—African Proverb

Affirmation

"I am Courageous."

Wisdom

"For the Lord giveth wisdom: out of his mouth cometh knowledge and understanding."

—Proverbs 2:6 | KJV

"Don't think there are no crocodiles just because the water is calm. "

—African Proverb

Wisdom

My mother was wise beyond her years. Her wisdom has guided many through good and bad times and is what many people miss most about her. No matter what your situation was she always had a sound piece of advice for you. It seemed as if she had lived several lifetimes during her stint here on this plane of existence. Her wisdom came largely through experience. These experiences often had her swimming in uncharted waters. The many lessons learned, and wisdom gained each time she made it to the other side helped her to navigate through life. The most important thing I learned from my mother about wisdom is to learn from the experiences of others. She would often say that "the worse kind of fool is an old fool!" This is because experience is and should be the best teacher.

Wisdom

The Word Says:

"See then that ye walk circumspectly, not as fools, but as wise, Redeeming the time, because the days are evil."

–Ephesians 5:15-16 | KJV

The Ancestors Say:

"Only a fool tests the depth of a river with both feet."

–African Proverb

Affirmation

"I use Wisdom in all matters!"

Wisdom

The Word Says:

"If any of you lack wisdom, let him ask of God, that giveth to all men liberally, and upbraideth not; and it shall be given him."

–James 1:5 | KJV

The Ancestors Say:

"A wise man never knows all, only fools know everything."

–African Proverb

Affirmation

"I use Wisdom in all matters!"

Wisdom

The Word Says:

"But the wisdom that is from above is first pure, then peaceable, gentle, and easy to be intreated, full of mercy and good fruits, without partiality, and without hypocrisy."

–James 3:17 | KJV

The Ancestors Say:

"A wise person does no fall down on the same hill twice."

–African Proverb

Affirmation

"I use Wisdom in all matters!"

Wisdom

The Word Says:

"How much better is it to get wisdom than gold! and to get understanding rather to be chosen than silver!"

–Proverbs 16:16 | KJV

The Ancestors Say:

"A fool cannot undo a knot tied by a wise man."

–African Proverb

Affirmation

"I use Wisdom in all matters!"

Wisdom

The Word Says:

"Say not thou, What is the cause that the former days were better than these? for thou dost not enquire wisely concerning this."

–Ecclesiastes 7:10 | KJV

The Ancestors Say:

"Knowledge without wisdom is like water in the sand."

–African Proverb

Affirmation

"I use Wisdom in all matters!"

Wisdom

The Word Says:

"Walk in wisdom toward them that are without, redeeming the time. Let your speech be always with grace, seasoned with salt, that ye may know how ye ought to answer every man."

—Colossians 4:5-6 | KJV

The Ancestors Say:

"Wisdom is wealth."

—African Proverb

Affirmation

"I use Wisdom in all matters!"

Wisdom

The Word Says:

"Only by pride cometh contention: but with the well advised is wisdom."

—Proverbs 13:10 | KJV

The Ancestors Say:

"Wisdom does not come overnight."

—African Proverb

Affirmation

"I use Wisdom in all matters!"

Wisdom

The Word Says:

"He that getteth wisdom loveth his own soul: he that keepeth understanding shall find good."

—Proverbs 19:8 | KJV

The Ancestors Say:

"The owl is the wisest of all birds because the more it sees the less it talks."

—African Proverb

Affirmation

"I use Wisdom in all matters!"

Wisdom

The Word Says:

"Who is a wise man and endued with knowledge among you? let him shew out of a good conversation his works with meekness of wisdom."

—James 3:13 | KJV

The Ancestors Say:

"The wise create proverbs for fools to learn not repeat."

—African Proverb

Affirmation

"I use Wisdom in all matters!"

Wisdom

The Word Says:

"So teach us to number our days, that we may apply our hearts unto wisdom."

—Psalm 90:12 | KJV

The Ancestors Say:

"If you are filled with pride then you will have no wisdom."

—African Proverb

Affirmation

"I use Wisdom in all matters!"

Forgiveness

"If my people, which are called by my name, shall humble themselves, and pray, and seek my face, and turn from their wicked ways; then will I hear from heaven, and will forgive their sin, and will heal their land."

—2 Chronicles 7:14 | KJV

"If you offend ask for pardon, if offended forgive."

—African Proverb

Forgiveness

Forgiveness was something my mother struggled with. Many of her family relationships were wrought with tension and a lack of forgiveness. It is hard to forgive someone when you feel as if they have committed unforgiveable acts. With time she learned that holding on to wrongs committed against you only causes damage. Not being able to let go of things damages your heart, mind and many times your soul. My mother's lessons on forgiveness were taught through how she learned to let go. She let go of the need to have apologies or admittance of wrongs committed. My most important take away about forgiveness is that you must first forgive yourself.

Forgiveness

The Word Says:

"And be ye kind one to another, tenderhearted, forgiving one another, even as God for Christ's sake hath forgiven you."

–Ephesians 4:32 | KJV

The Ancestors Say:

"He who forgives ends the quarrel."

–African Proverb

Affirmation

"I will Forgive."

Forgiveness

The Word Says:

"Forbearing one another, and forgiving one another, if any man have a quarrel against any: even as Christ forgave you, so also do ye."

—Colossians 3:13 | KJV

The Ancestors Say:

"The axe forgets, the tree remembers."

—African Proverb

Affirmation

"I will Forgive."

Forgiveness

The Word Says:

"Judge not, and ye shall not be judged: condemn not, and ye shall not be condemned: forgive, and ye shall be forgiven."

—Luke 6:37 | KJV

The Ancestors Say:

"People who love one another do not dwell on each other's mistakes."

—African Proverb

Affirmation

"I will Forgive."

Forgiveness

The Word Says:

"Then came Peter to him, and said, Lord, how oft shall my brother sin against me, and I forgive him? till seven times? Jesus saith unto him, I say not unto thee, Until seven times: but, Until seventy times seven."

—Matthew 18:21-22 | KJV

The Ancestors Say:

"Those who do not forgive break the bridge on which they have to pass."

—African Proverb

Affirmation

"I will Forgive."

Forgiveness

The Word Says:

"For thou, Lord, art good, and ready to forgive; and plenteous in mercy unto all them that call upon thee."

—Psalm 86:5 | KJV

The Ancestors Say:

"Forgive others not because they deserve forgiveness but because you deserve peace."

—African Proverb

Affirmation

"I will Forgive."

Forgiveness

The Word Says:

"And when ye stand praying, forgive, if ye have ought against any: that your Father also which is in heaven may forgive you your trespasses."

—Mark 11:25 | KJV

The Ancestors Say:

"When you forgive you don't change the past, you change the future."

—African Proverb

Affirmation

"I will Forgive."

Forgiveness

The Word Says:

"In whom we have redemption through his blood, the forgiveness of sins, according to the riches of his grace."

−Ephesians 1:7 | KJV

The Ancestors Say:

"Some give and forgive, others get and forget."

−African Proverb

Affirmation

"I will Forgive."

Forgiveness

The Word Says:

"And forgive us our debts, as we forgive our debtors."

–Matthew 6:12 | KJV

The Ancestors Say:

"If God were not forgiving heaven would be empty."

–African Proverb

Affirmation

"I will Forgive."

Forgiveness

The Word Says:

"And whosoever speaketh a word against the Son of man, it shall be forgiven him: but whosoever speaketh against the Holy Ghost, it shall not be forgiven him, neither in this world, neither in the world to come."

—Matthew 12:32 | KJV

The Ancestors Say:

"He who does not know is forgiven by God."

—African Proverb

Affirmation

"I will Forgive."

Forgiveness

The Word Says:

"Blessed is he whose transgression is forgiven, whose sin is covered."

–Psalm 32:1 | KJV

The Ancestors Say

"If you forgive the fox for stealing your chickens he will take your sheep."

–African Proverb

Affirmation

"I will Forgive."

Peace

"The Lord bless thee, and keep thee: The Lord make his face shine upon thee, and be gracious unto thee: The Lord lift up his countenance upon thee, and give thee peace."

—Numbers 6:24-26 | KJV

"When there is no enemy within the enemies outside cannot hurt you."

—African Proverb

Peace

The tenth and final pillar that represents who my mother was is Peace. She lived her life in a manner where she always tried to have peace. Every situation that was not peaceful she quickly worked to change. Sometimes this meant changing her physical location, at other times this meant cutting people off or ending situations. She provided a peaceful home where I always felt safe. The sense of peace that she instilled in me has helped me to flourish. What she taught me about peace is very simple. Anything that costs you your peace is too expensive.

Peace

The Word Says:

"These things I have spoken unto you, that in me ye might have peace. In the world ye shall have tribulation: but be of good cheer; I have overcome the world."

–John 16:33 | KJV

The Ancestors Say:

"Peace is costly but is worth the expense."

–African Proverb

Affirmation

"I will have Peace in my life!"

Peace

The Word Says:

"Peace I leave with you, my peace I give unto you: not as the world giveth, give I unto you. Let not your heart be troubled, neither let it be afraid."

–John 14:27 | KJV

The Ancestors Say:

"If you can't resolve your problems in peace you can't solve war."

–African Proverb

Affirmation

"I will have Peace in my life!"

Peace

The Word Says:

"Blessed are the peacemakers: for they shall be called the children of God."

—Matthew 5:9 | KJV

The Ancestors Say:

"A soft word causes anger to turn back, a humble heart settles quarrels."

—African Proverb

Affirmation

"I will have Peace in my life!"

Peace

The Word Says:

"For he that will love life, and see good days, let him refrain his tongue from evil, and his lips that they speak no guile: Let him eschew evil, and do good; let him seek peace, and ensue it."

—1 Peter 3:10-11 | KJV

The Ancestors Say:

"There can be no peace without understanding."

—African Proverb

Affirmation

"I will have Peace in my life!"

Peace

The Word Says:

"I will both lay me down in peace, and sleep: for thou, Lord, only makest me dwell in safety."

—Psalm 4:8 | KJV

The Ancestors Say:

"The more you spend on peace the less you spend on war."

—African Proverb

Affirmation

"I will have Peace in my life!"

Peace

The Word Says:

"Thou wilt keep him in perfect peace, whose mind is stayed on thee: because he trusteth in thee."

—Isaiah 26:3 | KJV

The Ancestors Say:

"Don't celebrate war, cry or peace."

—African Proverb

Affirmation

"I will have Peace in my life!"

Peace

The Word Says:

"Depart from evil, and do good; seek peace, and pursue it."

−Psalm 34:14 | KJV

The Ancestors Say:

"A man who never recognizes his mistakes will never know peace."

−African Proverb

Affirmation

"I will have Peace in my life!"

Peace

The Word Says:

"Now no chastening for the present seemeth to be joyous, but grievous: nevertheless afterward it yieldeth the peaceable fruit of righteousness unto them which are exercised thereby."

–Hebrews 12:11 | KJV

The Ancestors Say:

"He who runs after good fortune runs away from peace."

–African Proverb

Affirmation

"I will have Peace in my life!"

Peace

The Word Says:

"Therefore being justified by faith, we have peace with God through our Lord Jesus Christ."

—Romans 5:1 | KJV

The Ancestors Say:

"Silence gives rise to peace and with peace comes security."

—African Proverb

Affirmation

"I will have Peace in my life!"

Peace

The Word Says:

"The Lord will give strength unto his people; the Lord will bless his people with peace."

—Psalm 29:11 | KJV

The Ancestors Say:

"A man with too much ambition cannot sleep in peace."

—African Proverb

Affirmation

"I will have Peace in my life!"

Mom,

I never imagined doing life without you. The pain I felt when you left us was indescribable. With much prayer and love from friends and family I have been able to pull it together just a little more each day. One of the things that everyone misses most about you is your advice. The words you have spoken over and into my life and the lives of countless others are priceless. Although many of us have tried, we will never replace the wisdom you gave us while here on earth. I have to admit I sometimes feel a bit lost without you here on the physical plane. This book although difficult to write was necessary. I have attempted to gather many of your reflections, prayers, meditations and affirmations in one place. You left the blueprint. We just need to follow the plan. Prayerfully you don't mind me sharing you with the world…

Signed,

The Daughter

Mom Said:
"ALL IS WELL!"

Mom you were always right...

CONNECT WITH RASHIDA TAHIRAH

Instagram

authorrashidatahirah

Facebook

Author Rashida Tahirah

Twitter

@rashidatahirah

Website

RashidaTahirah.com